The Cooking Star who owns this

book is ....

for messy kids

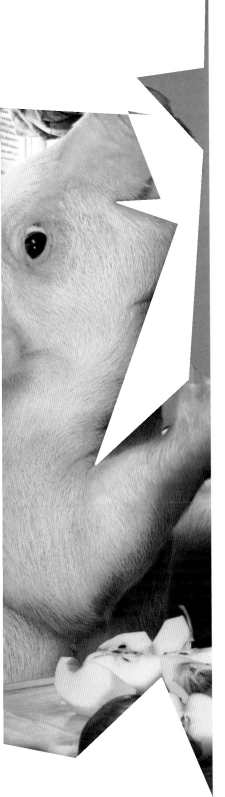

'Little Piglet' is an original
concept from the
Icarus 2009 Calendar
© Icarus Arts Publishing Limited

**Photography by
Steve Bicknell
Post Production Paul Cocken**

Concept - Steve Bicknell

Design - Georgina Cookson

**Cooking - Joan Shotnik
Shevon Burrows**

Maverick Arts Publishing Ltd
Studio 4 Hardham Mill Park
Pulborough
West Sussex RH20 1LA

©Maverick Arts Publishing Limited (2009)

PUBLISHED BY MAVERICK ARTS
PUBLISHING LTD

ISBN 978-1-84886-001-8

Maverick
arts publishing

www.maverickartsclub.com

Little Piglet

cookbook

for messy kids

Fun, Healthy Vegetarian Recipes

Easy to cook and great to eat

Each recipe has a Mess Factor

9/10

Mess Factor

Blame our Little Piglet Cooking Stars!

Maverick

arts publishing

Our Cooking Stars

The piggy Jones family are enthusiastic cooks and want to pass on some of their favourite recipes that they cook in their family. The piglets all join in with you and have lots of fun. They all love making a mess, cleaning it up and best of all getting to eat what they have made at the end.

Billy

Billy loves being in the kitchen and tries to outsmart his family all the time. He is always the fastest to the kitchen and likes mixing, whisking and washing up! He is always inventing jokes and up to something silly with his older brother Harry!

Rosie

Being the youngest has its advantages! As Rosie knows, you can be the messiest without getting told off. Her favourite colour is pink so when she gets a chance to choose, it's always - strawberry jelly and pink icing.

Ruby

Being arty, Ruby loves colourful puddings and her favourite is the knicker-trota-glory. She loves to make up new combinations and is trying to use chocolate and peanut butter in her new version! "You can never have too many toppings" says Ruby.

Poppy

Poppy loves chopping and making shapes for soups and dippers. She is fast and neat but also loves jokes, surprises and food fights with the boys. She the first to run away when Mum wants the washing up done!

As the oldest boy Harry is a little bigger and tougher than the rest of the piglets. His strength means he is excellent at making dough, frying and grating cheese (although he eats it along the way). He gets into trouble with his little brother Billy but often takes the blame!

Harry

3

Iced Biscuits

Ingredients:

100g/3½oz unsalted butter, softened

100g/3½oz caster sugar

1 egg

275g/10oz plain flour

2 drops vanilla essence

To decorate:
400g/14oz icing sugar

3-4 different food colourings

small sweets
glace cherries

Utensils:

Wooden spoon
2 Bowls
2 Forks
Sieve
Biscuit cutters

How to make:

1 Beat the butter with a wooden spoon until soft.

2 Add the sugar to the butter and beat again until it is light and fluffy.

3 Whisk the egg in a separate bowl with a fork and then add gradually to the butter and sugar, beating all the time.

4 Add the flour and vanilla essence. Mould the mixture into a ball with your hands.

5 Lightly flour the work surface and roll out the dough until it's about the thickness of a one pound coin. Use cutters to make shapes (stars, hearts, etc). Lift on to a baking sheet.

6 Bake the biscuits for 8-10 minutes at 190C/375F/Gas 5. Leave to harden for a couple of minutes, then put on a wire rack to cool.

7 For the icing, sift the icing sugar into a large bowl and gradually add enough hot water to make a soft, firm mixture - about 2-3 tablespoons.

8 Divide the icing into 3 or 4 bowls and add ½ tsp of colouring to each one. Be careful not to mix the colours! Spread the icing onto the biscuits with a table knife and decorate.

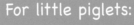

For little piglets:
You can decorate in lots of ways.
Loads of fun, very messy but pretty.

4

Rosie's got it licked!

Rosie's lovely and messy!

Gingerbread Piglets

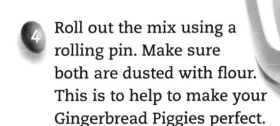

9/10
Mess Factor

How to make:

1. Put the flour, butter, ground ginger and bicarbonate of soda into a big mixing bowl.

2. Mix it all together until it feels like crumbs.

3. Add the sugar, syrup and egg and mix it with a spoon until it forms into a soft lump which feels like plastercine. (You can lick the syrup off the tablespoon, if Mum says it's OK)

For little piglets:
See if you can name each little piglet you have made!

4. Roll out the mix using a rolling pin. Make sure both are dusted with flour. This is to help to make your Gingerbread Piggies perfect.

5. Now get your piggy shaped stencils out and press very hard onto the flattened pastry lump until you can see small piggies in the mix.

6. Ask a big piglet to grease a baking tray. Now with your fingers gently place the cut out Piggies onto the tray.

7. A big piglet now has to go and preheat the oven to 180C/350F/Gas Mark 4. Cook for 15 minutes or until golden brown. Delicious!

Ingredients:

350g plain flour

100g butter

1 teaspoon of ground ginger

1 teaspoon bicarbonate of soda

150g of light soft brown sugar

4 tablespoons of golden syrup

1 medium egg

Utensils:

Measuring bowl

Rolling pin

Piggy stencil or your own shapes

Mixing bowl

Wooden spoon

Pastry board

Baking tray

Utensils:

Saucepan

Slotted spoon

Eggcup

Plate

Knife

Teaspoon

Eggy Soldiers

Mess Factor 1/10

How to make:

1 Fill the saucepan with water to 3/4 full from the top (Ask someone to help lift the pan).

2 Choose your eggs. If they are ok they will sink in the water.

3 Firstly (ask for help turning the heat on), place your chosen eggs in the saucepan and bring the water to the boil.

4 Wind the timer to 3 minutes or use a stop watch. Put some bread in the toaster.

5 When the timer rings carefully scoop out the eggs with the slotted spoon. Be careful they will be VERY hot!

6 Butter your toast and cut into soldiers. Put your egg in the eggcup. Ask Mum to cut off the top. Enjoy!

For little piglets:

When you have eaten your egg, turn it round and draw your own piggie face on the shell.

Billy's a smash hit!

Billy's a Wizz!

Blueberry Yogurt Muffins

How to make:

8/10
Mess Factor

1 Preheat the oven to 180C/ 350F/Gas Mark 4.

2 Separate the eggs and mix yolks with the maple syrup. Beat in the flour and bicarbonate of soda, then the yogurt, lemon zest and lemon juice until thoroughly blended. Add in most of the blueberries, saving some for decoration.

3 Whisk the egg whites in a separate bowl until stiff. Fold them into the yogurt mixture.

4 Place the muffin cases into the Yorkshire pudding tray. Add the mixture two cm from the top and add the remaining blueberries as decoration.

5 Bake in the oven for 30 minutes until the muffins have risen and the top is brown. Allow to cool and gobble up.

Ingredients:

2 large free-range eggs, separated

50g maple syrup

250g wholemeal flour

1 teaspoon of bicarbonate of soda

200g strained Greek yogurt

Zest and juice of half a lemon

100g blueberries

Butter, for greasing

Utensils:

Yorkshire pudding tray

Mixing bowl

Scoop or large serving spoon

Muffin cases

For little piglets:
Makes 10-12 cakes, enough for all your school friends...

Knicker-trota-glory

Ingredients:

1/4 packet of red jelly

1/4 packet of yellow jelly

Can of sliced peaches

Can of pineapple chunks

Block of vanilla ice cream

1/4 pint of double cream (whipped)

Glace cherries

Utensils:

Tall sundae glasses

Bowls

Whisk and spoons

How to make:

1 Make up both the jellies and mash when set.

2 Put the peaches and pineapple in the bottom of the glasses.

3 Cover with a layer of red jelly, then a layer of ice cream followed by a layer of yellow jelly.

4 Repeat the layers leaving some space at the top.

5 Whip the cream in a bowl, then add to the top of the sundae. Finally add the cherries on top.

For little piglets:
Don't eat too many of those yummy cherries!

4/10

Mess Factor

Dig in Ruby!

 14

Poppy's getting warm!

A Super Soup!

How to make:

1 Melt the butter and fry the diced carrots, onion, potatoes and green pepper until softened.

2 Add 450ml (3/4 pint) water, lentils, salt, pepper and bay leaf and simmer for 30 minutes.

3 Mix the flour with a little of the milk and gradually blend in the rest. Stir well into the soup until it thickens. Simmer for 5 minutes then stir in 75g (3oz) cheese.

4 Pour into a serving dish, garnish with the remaining cheese and sprinkle with croutons. Serve immediately.

4/10

Mess Factor

For little piglets:
This is a great first recipe. Really tasty!

Ingredients:

1oz (25g) butter

1lb (450g) carrots, peeled and diced

1 medium onion, skinned and sliced

2 medium potatoes, peeled and diced

1 small green pepper, seeded and chopped

2oz (50g) lentils
salt and ground pepper

1/2 bay leaf

3/8 cup (40g) plain flour, sieved

3/4 pint (450ml) milk

4oz (100g) English Cheddar cheese, grated

Croutons to garnish

Utensils:

Saucepan

Frying pan

Sharp knife

Grater (for cheese)

Measuring jug

Chopping board

15

Ingredients:

Red jelly

Green jelly

Utensils:

Measuring jug

Fork

Jelly mould

Wooden spoon

Large plate

Wibbly Wobbly Jelly

How to make:

1 Make up the jellies as instructed on the packets.

2 Use the red jelly in the mould and leave to set. Be very careful with the boiling water.

3 Turn out the red jelly very carefully onto a large plate.

4 When the green jelly has set, mash it up with a fork and put it round the red jelly.

5 Bring into the party making sure it wobbles lots...

Wibbly wobbly fun!

For little piglets:

Make this with your friends and get Mum to judge who's the jelly winner!

2/10

Mess Factor

16

Ruby, the party animal!

17

Billy juggles with disaster!

Billy's Brill Apple Pie

How to make:

9/10 Mess Factor

1 Sieve the flours and a pinch of salt into a large mixing bowl. Add butter and rub lightly into the flour with your fingertips. Lift the mixture high above the bowl as you rub, to let air into the pastry and make it lighter. Continue until fine then stir in the sugar.

2 Lightly beat 1 egg with 1 tablespoon chilled water, then drizzle over the flour mixture. Start to bring the dough together to form into a smooth ball with your hands, adding a little more water if necessary.

3 Divide the dough into two pieces, wrap in cling film, and chill for 30 minutes. Peel and core the apples then cut each into 8 pieces. Mix with lemon juice in a large bowl. Place the butter and sugar in a large fry pan over a low heat. When the butter has melted, add apples and spices, then stir together.

4 Cook, stirring occasionally, for 10 minutes or until apples have softened. Set aside to cool.

5 **Pastry Base:** Roll out the larger pastry ball on a floured surface to a 30cm circle (about 2mm thick). Place into the pie dish and gently press into corners, allow excess to overhang. Place filling in base with a slotted spoon.

6 **Pastry Top:** Roll the small pastry piece to a 25cm circle. Add to the base of the pie and crimp the edges with your fingers. Cut off excess pastry. Mix egg and milk to brush on the top and sprinkle with caster sugar. Cut four small air vents.

7 Preheat oven to 180C/350F/Gas Mark 4. Place pie dish on a baking tray and bake for 45 minutes or until golden brown.

Ingredients:

Pastry Crust:

1 3/4 cups (260g) plain flour

1/2 cup (75g) self-raising flour

185g unsalted butter, chilled, cut into small pieces

1/3 cup (75g) caster sugar

2 eggs, 1 tbs milk
Caster sugar to sprinkle

Filling:

8 Granny Smith apples

Juice of 1 lemon

45g unsalted butter

1/2 cup (110g) caster sugar

1 tsp ground cinnamon

1/4 tsp ground cloves

Utensils:

Sieve, Mixing bowl

Large bowl, Pastry board

Pie dish, Frying pan

Knife, Pastry brush

Ingredients:

2 cups spiral pasta

1 cup sweetcorn

Large jar pasta sauce

1 cup milk

1 cup grated tasty cheese

Butter for greasing

Utensils:

Saucepan

Mixing bowl

Grater

Wooden spoon

Casserole dish

Cheesy Pasta Bake

How to make:

1 Cook dry pasta in boiling water until tender. Drain well and set aside.

2 In another pan mix the sweetcorn, pasta sauce and milk. Heat for 2-3 minutes.

3 Gently mix in the cooked pasta to the sauce. Spoon mixture into a greased casserole dish.

4 Sprinkle with grated cheese and bake in a preheated oven at 180C/350F/Gas Mark 4 for 20 minutes.

For little piglets:
Mind your fingers when grating the cheese!

5
/10
Mess Factor

That's grate Harry!

Rosie loves chocolate!

Little Piggie Crispie Cakes

How to make:

1 Melt the chocolate in a small bowl with the syrup over a bowl of boiling water.
Be very careful with the boiling water!

2 Add the rice crispies to the chocolate and mix well.

3 Divide the mixture between 12 cake cases.

4 Put them in the fridge to set.

5/10
Mess Factor

For big piglets:
Leave some for the kids!

Ingredients:

150g (6oz) dark chocolate

1 tablespoons of golden syrup

75g (3oz) Rice crispies

Utensils:

Bowl

Saucepan

Wooden spoon

Cake cases

23

Poppy's chilling out!

Vegetarian Rice Salad

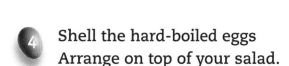

5
10

Mess Factor

How to make:

1. Arrange the lettuce on the platter.

2. Mix the rice and sweetcorn together and spoon into the centre of the platter.

3. Arrange the sliced cucumber in a circle on top of the rice. Repeat with grated carrot, peppers, and cheese, so that you have colourful salad.

4. Shell the hard-boiled eggs Arrange on top of your salad.

5. Serve with your favourite dressing, mayonnaise or salad cream.

Ingredients:

6 large romaine lettuce leaves

2 cups cooked rice

½ cup tinned sweetcorn

1 cup diced or sliced cucumber

1 cup diced green/red pepper

1 cup grated carrot

1 cup mild cheese cut into bite-sized cubes

3 hard-boiled eggs

Utensils:

Large platter dish

Knife

Spoon

For little piglets:
Carrots are lovely to eat raw!

25

Little Piggie Pizzas

Ingredients:

1 standard size bagel

Shredded mozzarella cheese

Tomato sauce

Toppings:

Diced green pepper, onion, chopped tomato or whatever you fancy!

Seasoning:
Basil, Oregano and Pepper

Utensils:

Baking sheet, knife

How to make:

1. Set the oven to a low heat.

2. Cut the bagel in half and spread tomato sauce on both inside halves.

3. Sprinkle the shredded cheese over the tomato sauce.

4. Prepare your toppings and arrange on top. Sprinkle on seasonings that you like best.

5. Put your bagels on o the baking sheet and bake in the oven on a low heat for 5 to 10 minutes.

6. The cheese will bubble up when your pizzas are ready.

7. Leave to cool down a little. Enjoy!

For little piglets:
Try lots of different combinations! Ever so tasty!

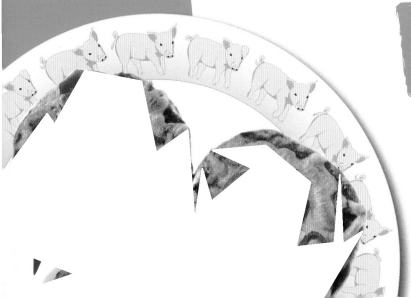

7/10

Mess Factor

Poppy loves a pizza!

Pig Sty stir fry!

Contains NUTS

Ingredients:

1 butternut squash

1 onion

Handful of runner beans

200g chick peas (or kidney beans or butter beans)

2 tbsp sesame oil (or vegetable oil)

2 tbsp sweet chilli sauce

OPTIONAL

2 tbsp peanut butter

1 egg

Utensils:

Potato peeler

Large wok or pan

A sharp knife

Chopping board

How to make:

4/10 Mess Factor

1. Peel the squash with a potato peeler. Chop off the stalk and flower end. Chop in half and use a spoon to remove the seeds. Chop into 1cm cubes.

2. Heat the sesame oil in a wok (or a large pan, if you don't have a wok)

3. Put the squash in the wok and cover. Cook for 5 minutes.

4. Peel the onion and slice it finely. Add it to the wok and cook for 2 minutes, stirring regularly.

5. Slice the runner beans into 1 cm chunks and add to the wok with the chick peas. Cook for 2 minutes.

6. When the vegetables are almost cooked, mix together with the sweet chilli sauce, the peanut butter (optional) and the egg (optional). Note: this sauce is thick - add a little water if you find it hard to mix.

7. Stir well for 2 minutes to make sure the egg is cooked. Serve and eat at once. Delicious!

For little piglets:

This stir fry is great on its own or served with noodles or rice.

Harry goes chinese!

Billy's all washed up!

Helping in the kitchen

1. Help set up the recipe by fetching all the different ingredients from the fridge or cupboard.

2. Wash all vegetables and fruit under the cold tap. Billy loves doing this as he likes to juggle everything dry!

3. Measuring the ingredients can be a very important job. With the help of an older piglet measure out exactly what you need. Ruby loves this job as she prides herself on getting everything perfect.

4. Be VERY careful when cutting up all your vegetables or fruit. You must ALWAYS ask an adult to help you!

5. Set the table before the whole family sits down to eat.

6. Washing up can be a fun thing to do with bigger piglets. The older piglet must begin washing all the messy plates, forks and spoons. Your job as the little piglet is to do the drying up. Grab yourself a clean tea towel and try your best to get things dry!

How to join the Maverick Arts Club

www.maverickartsclub.com

Login to the website to join and enjoy
special members offers

Other Maverick Children's Books...

WILLIE & NILLIE TAKE ON GONZALO

ISBN 978-1-84886-002-5

THE WORLD'S STRONGEST GUINEA PIG

This is the story of two guinea pig friends,
Willie and Nillie.
To enter the World's Strongest Guinea Pig
Competition, they have to go from slobs to
superfit guys in no time.
Come and join the furry friends on their
 mission to get strong
and fit to take on the
awesome Gonzalo.

ISBN 978-1-84886-000-1

FEARLESS FREDDIE
Beach Adventure

This is the story of Sarah and her best friend,
Fearless Freddie, who rescues Sarah with his
superskis on their beach holiday abroad.

arts publishing

Savoury Recipes

Mess Factor

34

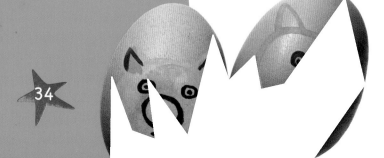